SICKLE CELL MANAGEMENT IN NIGERIA

Augusta Koroma

Contents

Dedication 4

Acknowledgement..5

Abstract 8

CHAPTER 1 11

   1.1 Introduction 11

   1.2 Sickle Cell Disease in Nigeria 21

Chapter Two..23

   2.0 Understanding Sickle Cell 23

   2.1 New Born screening 24

   2.2 Antenatal Screening 28

   2.3 Clinical care of prenatal screening 33

   2.4 Clinical treatment of Sickle cell disease 38

   2.5 Genetic Counseling 43

   2.6 Social Environment 48

Chapter 3 51

   3.1 Sickle Cell Findings 51

Chapter 4 69

4.1 Conclusion and Recommendation 69

4.2 Recommendation 76

References 78

Dedication

This book is dedicated to the victim of Sickle Cell in Nigeria

Acknowledgement

I acknowledge my family and supporters that encourage me to be more active on sickle cell

@ 2019 – Sickle Cell Management in Nigeria

This publication is designed to provide accurate and authoritative information in regard to the subject matter covered.

It is sold with the understanding that the publisher is not engaged in rendering legal or other professional service. If legal advice or other expert assistance is required, the services of a competent professional should be sought.

Copyright © 2019

All rights reserved

Printed in the United States of America

ISBN - 978-0-244-48019-6

No part of this book may be used or reproduced in any manner whatsoever without written permission except in the case of brief quotations embodied in critical articles and reviews.

For more information about the author, conference speaking engagement and purchase of bulk copies of this book visit -

info@sicklecellintervention.co.uk

First Edition

Abstract

The issue of sickle cell disease is a global health phenomenon and the regions of the sub-Saharan Africa have seen muchimpact of this disease with Nigeria carrying the highest burden.

Despite the significant progress made in the developed countries such as the UK and the US as a result of early screenings of newborn and antenatal programs, pharmacological and non-pharmacological therapies, intensive care and bone marrow transplant, which has reduced the rate of mortality and morbidity and have also positively impacted the quality of lives of carriers, it is sad to notethat the management in

Africa and in Nigeria to be precise has been described as suboptimal with reasons identified.

Methodology and Result

The literature searches were carried out to identify researches conducted between the years 2007 till date, aiming at examining the management of sickle cell disease and its limitations in Nigeria. Eleven studies were authenticated and reviewed. The result revealed that, the management of sickle cell in the global scene is multifocal and therefore applying this in the Nigerian context, six areas were considered, and these are; newborn screening, Antenatal screening, clinical care of prenatal screening, clinical treatment of sickle cell disease, genetic counseling and the social environment, with each limitation identified.

Conclusion

The management of sickle cell disease in Nigeria is considered very significant and therefore must and therefore policy makers and practitioners must work to make sure the prevalence of the disease in Nigeria can be minimized in relation to the developed countries.

CHAPTER 1

1.1 Introduction

Sickle cell disease (SCD) is described as a genetic disorder that patient inherent from both parents, and it portraysan irregular red blood cell that forms a sickled shape.

This reduces the flexibility of the red cell amounting to the destruction and interference with the normal free flow of red blood in the molecule resulting in low oxygen, and with complications as outcome and this can lead to extreme back pain, chest pain, hands and feet. It could also cause damage to bones, muscles and organs. People that are associated with this disorder in most cases feel weak, tired and pale looking (WHO, 2017).

The World Health Organization (WHO, 2017) estimated about 5% as potential carriers of this trait globally, which is majorly in SCD and thalassemia, and over 300,000 babies are born with it annually. This disorder shortens the life expectancy of a carrier as it also accountable for about 50% of mortality rate in Africa (Piet et al., 2013) and Africa alone recording more than 200,000 cases with its health implication of either death or disability.

In Nigeria for instance, with an estimated population of about 180 million, it is indicated that about 24% representing about 40million of the Nigerian population have the trait of the disorder and the occurrence of sickle-cell anaemia is in the ratio of 24 to 1000 births (Akinyanju, 2015; WHO, 2017).

This shows that more than 100,000-150,000 children are born annually in Nigeria with prevailing sickle cell anaemia, henceMolineauxet al., (1979) cited in Akinyaju, (2015) stated that,

"There is no other known inherited disorder present at such frequency in a large population and of comparable severity as sickle cell anaemia in Africa.With rising standards of living and control of malaria, sickle cell anaemia will become an immense medical, social and economic problem throughout the continent"

It is further noted that the survival of the children born with the disorder beyond childhood is reliant on the provision and access to proper care and this can only be possible with an effective management and preventive programs (WHO, 2017).

To this effect, WHO in its 59th assembly in 2006, call on the affected countries globally to strengthen their response to the ailment, and an adoption on the prevention and management of SCD and thalassemia's was initiated. This is to increase the awareness of the burden globally, the promotion of equal access to medical services, providing technical support for prevention and management and the promotion and supporting of research in improving the quality of life of the affected (WHO, 2017).

Famuyiwa (2015) indicated that apart from the primary physical constraints, sickle cell disease is fraught with psychological and emotional issues which must be reduced to guarantee a much better life, as theaffected who exhibit expected control over the impact of the disorder and those who could manage and get the best of life could achieve an enviable height. However, Steinberg (1999) noted that basic and clinical investigation has been the major factor for the improvement in the way of life of patients in the developed countries, which has led to a significant rise in the life expectancy of patients, whereas in Africa where the chief burden lies, minimal standard of care is not available.

With the increasing burden therefore, it is considered imperative to have a basic understanding of how the disorder is managed.

According to Humphrey (2012), the management of SCD could be classified as multifocal, multidisciplinary approach that requires a collaborative effort between carrier, family and health care team. However, WHO (2005) noted that most countries where sickle-cell anaemia is prevalent, the management has remained insufficient, lack of control programs, lack of basic facilities to manage the patients, the screening processes are not a common practice and issues to diagnosis are only implemented when a patient comes with a severe difficulty. Cheap and cost-effective measures like the usage of penicillin to avoid infections are not reachable to large number of carriers in many countries and in Nigeria to be specific where the disorder is prevalent, it is indicated that most carriers live in rural settlement and the level of care of both tertiary and secondarycenters are suboptimal (Adekile, 2017)

This disturbance has stimulatedmany Nigerians to implement actions about sickle cell ailment, however, what needed to be implemented often emerge misleading and not properly and fully reasoned and therefore remain an issue of confusion and controversy among health care practitioners (Akinyaju, 2015).

To this respect, the common issue that comes up would be the one of how the disorder will be completely eradicated while the management and treatment in the wider context is invariably ignored. Hence the sickle cell foundation in Nigeria was registered in 1994 with a vision and mission of developing a world class center, driving for the search for an impactful solution and to alleviate the burden of sickle cell disorder to ensure that all affected can live pain free lives.

The outlined programs for the center includes; Genetic counseling, clinical services, prenatal diagnosis, reference laboratory services, library and information services, stroke prevention and leg ulceration treatment (SCFN,2015).

Despite this, Adekile cited in Ogundipe (2017) noted that the chunk of the crisis still lies with the government, in the sense that, the action of the government towards the control and management has been that of "lip service" and therefore it is believe that not until the government comes up with proper policies in the management of the disorder, much impact will not be felt.

The world health organization (WHO, 2005) stated that, to improve the prospect of the patients in the developing countries, the main focus should be on early involvement for avoidable difficulties with pain medication, antibiotics, nutrition, folic acid supplementation and high fluid intake, and it was further noted that in the past decade, there has been remarkable progress in various respect such as long term management with hydroxyurea which has reduced the rate pain associated crisis and the improvement in the quality of life of patients, imaging studies, helping with instant management of complications such as stroke and chest syndrome, bone marrow transplant and blood transfusion.

However, Yawn and John-Sowah (2015) noted that both hydroxyurea and blood transfusion are presently underused and are not monitored or carried out by family physicians and in Nigeria, McBaun (2013) however suggested that given the large numbers of sickle cell carrier, hydroxyurea may not be feasible at the initial time, but a targeted technique for the use of hydroxyurea as an option to the standard treatment for high risk patients. It is worth noting that, advances in medical health which are primarily applicable in highresource countries, are far from reach in the developing countries and have unfortunately broaden the differences between patients in developed and developing countries in terms of quality of life, and it is therefore believe that these differences can only be minimized through generic upgrading in health care services, but the question arises as to why there are underutilization of medicines and lack of proper management in Africa and Nigeria specifically.

To this end, this systematic research work tends to identify the factors militating against the effectiveness of the management techniques for sickle cell disease in Nigeria in impacting the quality of life of Sickle cell patients.

1.2 Sickle Cell Disease in Nigeria

In Nigeria today to be specific, with a high prevalence rate of 24% accounting for about 40million Nigerians as carriers of the sickle cell disease, and with an estimated figure of about 150,000 new born babies with sickle cell disease annually and with a further estimation of only 5% of such birth surviving past a decade as compared to 96% surviving into adulthood in the United State and United Kingdom (Alege, 2015; Armstrong, N/A), it now become imperative to review and examine the level of Sickle Cell Management across all levels of health care in the Country, and to enforce a comprehensive approach to the prevention and management of the disorder.

Furthermore, it is stated that at present, many the affected in Nigeria do not receivesattention or care for this disorder.This research is therefore being imminent to enable, public Health practitioners and policy writers alike to develop the necessary intervention that is required to address Sickle Cell Care Management in Nigeria.

Chapter Two

2.0 Understanding Sickle Cell

This chapter forms the study guide to this dissertation, as it gives the ability to review what has been said by different authors with respect to the management of sickle cell globally and Nigeria specifically. Emphasis will be on the six chosen key management techniques, these include;

- New born screening
- Antenatal screening
- Clinical care of prenatal screening

- Clinical treatment of sickle cell disease
- Genetic counseling
- Social environment

2.1 New Born screening

According to the sickle cell foundation Nigeria (SCFN, 2017), the new born screening is designed for early diagnosis and identification of affected children with sickle disease, this will enable a proper referral and interventions to prevent avertable mortality and burden.

Literatures have revealed that life threatening complications of sickle cell diseases such as, sepsis, splenic sequestration crisis and so on can be avoided if only the early diagnosis is carried out within the first 3-6months of a child's life andwith the use of simple but impactful prophylacticprocedures such as;Penicillin and vaccination, indicatively will reduce morbidity and mortality in newborn with sickle cell disease (Lane,2001; Frommel et al., 2014). This has been proven by the clear reduction in the advance countries of mortality rate from 16% to less than 1% (Odunvbun, et al., 2008).

In the same vein, early demonstration shows that when newborn screening is linked to early diagnostic exercise, parental education and an extensive care and follow up, will reduce morbidity and mortality rate significantly in sickle cell disease in early childhood (Vichinsky, et al., 1988).

In a research carried out in Quebec in Canada between the years 1988-2003, of 9619 newborns, it was identified that 10.5% of children were at riskof sickle cell trait and 0.4% were diagnosed of the disease HbSS and were immediately enrolled and referred to a multidisciplinary sickle cell follow up clinic, another 0.4% had HbSC and appropriate medical attention were given within 10 weeks of diagnosis (Robitaille,et al., 2006).

DeBaun and Galadanci (2017) however, indicated that laboratory methods to facilitate newborn screening require infrastructure and facilities, and such are not routinely available in Africa and Nigeria in specific.

This however corroborates the work of McGann et al., (2016) who noted that, the screening capacity is limited in Africa, and currently in Nigeria, there is lack of newborn screening program (Adewoyin, 2015).

Suboptimal laboratory support in developing countries does not permit health care practitioners to complete and confirm diagnosis (Jain et al., 2015). The uses of High Performance Liquid Chromatography (HPLC), isoelectric focusing (IEF) or Capillary zone electrophoresis (CZE) are irregular and too costly to afford. These infrastructures they said are reliable but need huge financial investment and ongoing cost of maintenance, but not sufficient for all Africa countries.

Hence Piety et al., (2017) highlighted some of the complication with low resource economies of sub- Saharan African hindering the conventional implementation of newborn screening.

These they listed as; cost of materials too high, difficulty and dependence on electricity, expert equipment and provision related with normal diagnostic techniques, such as; high-performance liquid chromatography (HPLC) or isoelectric focusing electrophoresis(IEF), and their reliance on expert equipment, steadyinfrastructure and skilled laboratory workers.

For these reasons, newborn screening is restricted to few specialized laboratories in major places with majority of infants left out in the process.

2.2 Antenatal Screening

Antenatal diagnosis is the service which enables expectant parents who are carriers of the unusual disorder to find out early in pregnancy the likelihood of their unborn child having sickle cell anemia. With an early intervention possibly 10 weeks of pregnancy, which allows for early appropriate care, there is every tendency of preventing and reducing the frequency of the disorder or untimely death and to reduce childhood morbidity for the disorder (NHS, 2011; SCFN, 2015).

This is normally carried out by polymerase chain reaction with combination of enzyme detection of mutation and oligonuceid hybridization and in Nigeria, the foundation offers prenatal screening in three areas such as; Fetal blood sampling, Chorionic Villus Sampling (CVS) and Amniocentesis (SCFN, 2015).

Literature advocate the need for an early prenatal diagnosis, as it enables pregnant women to have more time and to take an informed decision about available options if the need be(BMJ, 2010).ROCG (2011) emphasized on the need for the use of Antenatal screening as it has significantly reducedmaternal morbidity and mortalityrate in SCD carriers during pregnancy because of better knowledge of the pathophysiology of the ailment and physiologic changethrough pregnancy. Despite the advances in the resourceful countries, the impact of prenatal screening is still very small. Jain et al., (2015) Wang et al., study, carried out a prenatal screening for SCD in 500 expectant mothers; it was observed that 51% opted for termination of pregnancies, and affected pregnancies with anemia and thalassemia fetus was 12%.

However, this study contradicts of Adewoyin (2015), who indicated that in Nigeria, prenatal diagnosis and selective abortion are controversial and not comparably available and that proportion of Nigerians will not opt for abortion even if legal. Atkin et al., (2008), however stated that when couples take decision on prenatal screening and termination of pregnancy, they do not only consider culture but also their faith and religion.

The national guideline for the control and management of sickle cell in Nigeria emphasized on the need for a multidisciplinary approach which must consist of Hematology doctor and nurses, Obstetrician and midwives,

Genetic counselors, Laboratory sickle cell expert, Psychologists, and Anesthetist. This will help in delivering the right information to increase awareness about procedures and therefore can influence screening and other related services.

Despite the huge benefit of this technique, there are drawbacks associated. Marteauet al., (2012) in theirfindings, it was revealed that expectant motherswelcomed the idea of early diagnosis, however the authors expresses preferences during the screening process with reference to multicultural context as this will influence perception and experiences with reference to acceptability of result.

In the same vein, Sinou (2017) stated that cultural and moral issues are positively correlated with the decision made on screening result. Furthermore, Fadare (2009) stresses on the implications of ethical concern because of possible abortion with fetuses having SS genotype which is part of the prenatal screening, such decision he described as difficult because they involved psychosocial, religious and cultural issues. Animasahun and Nwodo (2012), stresses on the lack of awareness among health care workers of prenatal screening in Nigeria and religion was noted as the major reason militating against its acceptability.

2.3 Clinical care of prenatal screening

Vichinsky (2017) noted that, majority of pregnancies with SCD related difficulties are most likely to result in livebirth and therefore are at a high danger of obstetrical and fetal difficulties and medical complications of sickle cell disease.

The associated risks are partly because of metabolic demands, hypercoagulable state and vascular stasis linked to pregnancy. In line with this, Lockwood and Magriples (2017) advocated the need for a prenatal care, with the goal of helping to ensure healthy baby at birth while reducing the risk to the mother. Such help will lead to; early, accurate judgment of gestation age, to identify pregnancies at high risk for mothers or fetal morbidity and mortality and continuous evaluation of mothers and fetal health status.

Ikeanyi and Ibrahim (2014) saw the need for early and quality antenatal care (ANC) in preventing maternal anemia and this they said cannot be overemphasized. Good nutrition awareness and practices or better prenatal services and the use of these services among well interested and concerned women that are well informed are expected to decrease the occurrence of the disease in pregnancy in any society, however, nutritional and best practices in Nigeria are still evolving.

Improved women awareness, health education, women empowerment, regular visitation to antenatal clinic attendance defaulters, encouragement and balanced diet are among factors listed that could lead to an effective utilization of prenatal interventions. For this to be implemented, Vichinsky (2017) emphasize the need for a knowledgeable multidisciplinary care team and high-risk obstetrics, which includes; one on one care, group prenatal care, subspecialty obstetrical care.

His work also corroborated the work of Odunvbun and Okolo (2015) who emphasized on the need for multi-disciplinary approach which offers a holistic attitude towards SCD care for children.

The management of sickle cell disease is posed with a lot challenges in Nigeria, such challenges not only associated with patients who do not only have the knowledge and awareness in some cases, but also the health care providers, who may not be familiar with current ideas in its management (Odunvbun and Okolo, 2015).

Literatures indicate that, most of best practices are being ignored; hence the prevalence of the disease on expected mothers and therefore inefficient management of the disease.

Factors such as, lack of compliance to best practice, mother's age, education, uniformity, cultural belief, ignorance, socioeconomic deprivation (poverty and low standard of living) or overconfidence to access facilities are most likely (Ndukwu and Dienye, 2012; Ikeanyi and Ibrahim, 2014).

Malnutrition has been described as a risk factor in children with the disease, and it increases the level of the disease (Jain and Colah, 2015).

Adewoyin and Obiechie advocate the need for expertise commitment together with wide array of therapeutic and prophylactic measures.

Therefore, a follow up to literature and national guidelines with reference to prenatal clinical care will help in lessening the burden of SCD patients and the unborn child.

2.4 Clinical treatment of Sickle cell disease

The treatment of sickle cell disease entails having routine test in monitoring health, pain management crises and treating associated health difficulties as they emerge. Sickle cell disease as it is having no general available cure; however available treatment can only help in avoiding crisis, relieving symptoms and lessening of complication (Emechebe et al., 2017).

In treating crisis, self-home treatment could be administered, where the patient can have proper bed rest, oral hydration, heat massaging, analgesia and other cognitive conducts (Rees et al., 2003), however, when self-treatment fails, then the emergency department can be an option.

Pharmacologic treatment intervention includes; nonopioid analgesics, such as; acetaminophen and nonsteroidal anti-inflammatorymedicine (NSAIDs); ibuprofen (10mg/kg for adults in every 6-8 hr.) and aspirin and possibly opioidalongside pain medicationsdaily, and in case of severity in some cases hospitalization.

In the case of anemia, blood transfusion can be used, while for infection, antibiotics and in rare cases, blood transfusions. For Acute chest syndrome, treatments emerge depending on the cause, and this could include; oxygen, medicine for infection treatment and to open airways for air improvement and blood transfusion. For Splenic Sequestration, the treatment is mostly blood transfusion and for vision loss, laser treatment can help if the retina is affected.

Leg Ulcers, could be treated with medicated creams, strong pain relievesand culture skin grafts in specialized centers can be used.

For stroke and Deep Vein Thrombosis and Pulmonary Embolism, the use of blood transfusion and medication are used respectively for treatment, and for hand foot syndrome, treatment usually will include pain medicine and increasing fluid intake (CDC, 2017).

However, literature indicates that in Nigeria, pharmacotherapeutic treatment choices for the disease have been very scarce in relation to the management of patients with and without painful (Ilesanmi, 2013) crises. Bone marrow treatment is described as the only cure currently for SCD, however finding the right donor is difficult and the process is expensive

Regardless of these treatment practices, Ansong et al., (2013) indicated that differences in health care settings between the advance countries and lack of resource in developing countries come with difficulties that can impact the management and treatment options in developing countries. In the real sense, health care practitioners in developing countries encounter difficulties in the management of patients with SCD.

Nevertheless, knowing the ailment, the progression, and putting in place appropriate methods to prevent it are consequential to its management.

Furthermore, it was indicated that lack of functional laboratories, drugs, delays in treatment, weak laboratories support in institutions, lack of analyzers and lack of Radiological facilities have all led to the differences between the advance countries and that of the developing countries in managing SCD.

2.5 Genetic Counseling

According to SCFN (2015), genetic counseling is essential to the management of SCD. This can be described as a situation where SCD patient and family members possibly carriers are given an unbiased information necessary in enabling them making an informed decision on reproductive behavior and other related courses of action.

There are basic objectives of genetic counseling and these are;

- To communicate information effectively and accurately about SCD,

- to enable patient make informed decision about the disease as both his life and family are at high risk,

- to give assistance in patient decision making, to erase the misconceptions about the disease,

- to enable the patient air out his expectations, concerns and anxieties in line with the disease (Heading and Fieding, 1975), and Such information should be supportive, non-directive and confidential (Akinyaju, 2015).

Literature emphasized the need for genetic counseling as itdoes not only provide insight about the epidemiology of the ailment, but useful for health planning. It was also demonstrated that premarital counseling has a direct impact on the reduction in the prevalence of the disease (Aneke and Okocha, 2016).

In the work of Toni-Uebari and Inusa, (2009), it was revealed that leaders and faith of religious organization have the ability in influencing and accessing at risk patients in increasing awareness about sickle cell disease, the encouragement of health service usage and the drive for ethnic related blood donors

Memish and Saeedi (2011) in a six years study of premarital screening for hemoglobinopathies, it was observed that, there was a steady reduction from 32.9 to 9.0 per 1000 persons examined in Saudi Arabia, and a five-fold rise in voluntary cancellation of intended marriagesbecause of the associated risk in couples.

In a similar study, it was revealed that couples who had prior knowledge of the disease had more chances of averting high risk marriagesand the strengthening of existing screening and counseling was made significantin this case(Alswaidi, et al.,2012). Oludarei (2013) saw the need for the use public education on the responsibility of premarital genetic counseling, and further stresses on the usefulness of individuals on continuing the genotype screening.

Regardless, factors such as emotions, social or financial consequence of test result have all lead to couples laying back. With emotions, couples get angry, faced with depression, worried or guilty about result outcome (Akande, 2010).

In certain cases, genetic counseling creates fear among couple, because it can reveal information which can affect the possibility of getting married.

Akande, (2010) also emphasized on the lack of treatment strategy and lack of government policies and possibly misunderstanding of genetic information as necessary factors why genetic counseling as a form of management has not been effective.

However, Akinyanju et al., (1999) stresses the need for nationwide application of this program.Therefore, it is worth noting that the essence of genetic counseling is built around making an informed decision and it has played a prominent role in alleviating burden of SCD.

2.6 Social Environment

Because of unexplained variability associated with SCD, literatures have shown that environmental and social factors relate to such variability (Asnani, et al., 2017).

According to Tewari et al., (2015) Environmental factors such as; climate, air quality, socio-economics, exercise and infection could be held responsible for the differences between developing and developed countries.

The authors noted that the difference in weather, such as cold or wind leads to patient hospitalization with acute pain; however, patients could have a ray of hope with a higher concentration of atmospheric carbon monoxide. Piel et al., (2017) noted in their work that, environmental factors mostly meteorological are highly correlated with hospital admission than air pollutant.

For an effective management under social environment, Literatures have demonstrated the impact of social support from family members as a strong indicator for improvement in the quality of life and adjustment for children with sickle cell and adolescents (Imhonde, 2013; Sansom-daly, et al., 2012 and Valenzuela et al., 2013).

Grove et al., (2014) emphasized on the need for the use of multi-media communication connections to schools, teachers and children with the same disorder. It was observed in a survey of four participant that, while the participant where hospitalized, they missed mostly; family members, friends, video games, internet and television.

It was also revealed that nowadays, hospitals connect health care providers/workers and patients remotelyusing multi-media in the monitoring of pains and to remind them of treatment if the need be (Jacob et al., 2013; Crosby et al., 2012 and Valenzuela et al., 2013). From the literature review on the management of sickle cell, as outline from the beginning of this review, it should be noted that every management method is designed to achieve its objective and therefore, emphasis should be on how to improve the quality of life for sickle cell disease (SCD) patientsusing these factors as identified in the literature.

Chapter 3

3.1 Sickle Cell Findings

In this chapter, the findings and analysis are presented. The findings were extracted and processed in relation to the research problem as stated in chapter one of this dissertation. The two objectives in this dissertation drove the findings and the analysis.

The first objective was the examination of sickle cell management skills and method in the Nigerian health care settings, and second is to determine their effectiveness. Both objectives were achieved, and the findings are true reflection of merging theory and practice. There were six themes in this dissertation and the findings must be associated with each theme.

4.1 Studies that identify ineffective management of sickle through newborn screening in Nigeria

In a group study in Enugu state in the Eastern part of Nigeria to identify newborn at high risk for targeted screening, using cellulose acetate electrophoresis, with respect to self-awareness of the disease genotype, and consenting to genotype screening, Burnham-Marusich et al., (2016), revealed that only 50% of participants provided precise self-report and the efficacy of self-report was different between participant who reported having the disease at 61% accuracy as to 86% accuracy who decline not having the disease.

The study concludes that, low level of report accuracy on parental self-report combine with the occurrence of the disease could inhibit the effectiveness of targeted newborn screening.

Despite the occurrence of sickle cell disease in Nigeria, it is sad to note that, there is no established universal newborn screening in Nigeria.

This is justified in the work of Galadanci et al., (2013). To document facilities of dedicated SCD clinics in Nigeria, a survey was carried out in 18 clinics residence in 11 institutions.

It was revealed that, only 3 of the clinics have High Performance Liquid Chromatography (HPLC) installed but not in use, and no one had isoelectric focusing (IEF). This again was confirmed by DeBaun and Galadanci, (2017) who reiterated the lack of new newborn screening which require infrastructure and facilities, and such are not routinely available in Africa and Nigeria in specific. This also corroborates the work of McGann et al., (2016) who noted again that, the screening capacity is limited in Africa, and this is because of economic constraint (Mulumba and Wilson,

2015)and currently in Nigeria, there is lack of newborn screening program

4.2 Studies that identify factors for ineffective management of sickle cell disease through Antenatal screening in Nigeria

Animasahun and Nwodo, (2012) in their study to determine the level of awareness and acceptability among health care professionals, it was revealed that, 91.3% are basically aware of the ailment, 75.3% are aware that prevention of the ailment can be affected through prenatal screening.

However, 42.1% will not permit termination of pregnancy once diagnosed of the disease, and 79% of those will do this basically because of religious reasons. This justify the work of Atkin et al., (2008) which noted that when decision with respect to prenatal screening and termination of pregnancy is being taken, couples put their faith and religion into consideration.

This work also concluded that, there is a poor level of awareness of the availability of prenatal screening services among health care workers in Nigeria and that religion is a major factor hindering its acceptability.

In a bid to identify factors militating against the acceptability of prenatal screening in Anambra state in Nigeria among health care workers, Ibeagha and Ibeagha (N/A), involving a total of 450 participantstook part in a stratified random sampling; the result showed that knowledge and religion are the major issues militating against prenatal screening.

Adewoyin et al., (2015) in an assessment to determine the level of knowledge in relation to sickle cell disease among a cross section of new graduates in Nigeria and to also identify factor influencing knowledge. It was demonstrated that awareness level is high with about 94.6%, however the acceptability rate for prenatal screening was only 38.1%.

Most participants demonstrated moderate level of public health knowledge regarding SCD in Nigeria. Considering the relative lack of prenatal diagnostic services, and the acceptability rate for abortion was low.

4.3 Studies that identify factors for ineffective management of sickle cell through prenatal care in Nigeria

In a cross-sectional study to determine the occurrence of sickle cell anemia in pregnancy in Nigeria, Ndukwu and Dienye (2012) revealed that, there is a high prevalence of the disease in River state, and socio-economic status among the demographic factors examined, shows highcorrelation with the care of the disease. This study also is in line with the work of Ifeanyi and Ibrahim (2014), who identify poverty and low standard of living as factors militating against effective management of sickle cell disease in Nigeria

4.4 Studies that identify factors for ineffective management of sickle cell through Genetic counseling in Nigeria

In a descriptive study with 30 hospitals in Lagos Nigeria with 150 participants to evaluate genetic counseling awareness, Adeyemo et al., (2007) reported that a generic informal genetic counseling take place occasionally. About 86% of participants are totally aware and knowledgeable of genetic counseling, however only 30.3% had undergone or exposed to genetic counseling

In a cross sectional descriptive study in the University of Benin Nigeria involving 400 respondents, to determine the importance of premarital counseling, Omuemu et al., (2013) demonstrated that, approximately 99% of the respondents are aware of SCD, and 78.9% of them are aware of the effectiveness of genetic counseling in preventing and managing the disease.

The acceptability of genetic counseling was approximately 97% however; the study noted that there was no significant relationship between the acceptability of premarital genetic counseling on cultural and religious ground as about 91% and 96% respectively would not hold these factors accountable.

In a descriptive cross sectional study of about 290 participants, in Port-Harcourt south-south Nigeria, Gbeneol et al., (2015) revealed that, there is awareness of premarital screening as 72.76% of the 84.83% participants had premarital screening before getting married and

9% shows AS on both intending couple, however, 21.05% went ahead with their marriage with a reason of not willing to jettison their spouse and 75% of them holding on to their religion and faith that God will prevent them from having children with SCD.

4.5 Studies that Identify factors for ineffective management of sickle cell disease through Clinical treatment in Nigeria

In a longitudinal and descriptive study between January-December 2014 to determine the financial burden placed on households by SCD in Ekiti State Nigeria, Olatunya et al., (2015), examined 111(64 male, 47 females) children with the disease managed in the University hospital in the pediatric unit.

The result revealed that, the monthly income for each household ranges from; N12, 500-N330, 000 ($76 and $2,000), while health expenditure is between N2, 500 and N215, 000. 63 parents lost 1-48 working days to children ill health. 23 children parents had loan between the range of N6, 500 –N150, 000 ($39-$909) to clear off bills. The amount income spent on each child ranges from 0.38%-34.4%, with a bench mark of 10% to determine catastrophic health expenditure; it was observed that 20.7% of the examined household income went into health care expenditure.The implication here impact on patient, family members as the health care cost is on the high side (Mitchell et al., 2007).

In cross sectional study at the University of Ibadan between January-April 2009, to determine the pattern of contraceptive use, Okunola et al., (2010), revealed that despite the high awareness of contraceptives with the studied group, the occurrence of contraceptive use is low as compared to the studied population. This is because of perceived fear of the actual and the imaginary side effect of certain contraceptive techniques and relative short of access to product sources.

4.6 DISCUSSION

The findings from the studies have been able to identify some of the factors thathinder the successful implementation of a standardized management technique of sickle cell disease in Nigeria.

In this research work, there are six sub-sections that were considered, and findings are analyzed as follows. The management of sickle cell disease through antenatal screening and newborn has been described as an indication of early diagnosis of the disease of the unborn and newborn child, upon diagnosis, it is expected that the right referral and prevention should be made, however, in Nigeria, this has not been effective, and this has led to prevalence of the disease in the country. The findings from the studies revealed lack of accuracy of self-report, lack of facilities and infrastructure, economic constraint, lack of knowledge and lack of awareness and acceptability of the programs.

In the real sense, it is stated that for collection of information with respect to individual health, accurate self-report is important as it aid health risk factor, care management and for the utilization of health care services (Short et al., 2009).

The other findings on newborn screening show the impact of lack of facilities and infrastructure. Health care facilities and infrastructures are assumed as elements of physical, technical and structural worth of health care settings (Scholz et al., 2015). It is therefore believed that any shortfall from the real will negatively impact on the implementation of a successful management of SCD.

However, the findings suggest that these facilities and infrastructures are far from reach because of economic constraints. It is believed that the provision of health care facilities and infrastructure in any economy, is the responsibility of the government however in the case of Nigeria, the government involvement has been that of "lip service" (Adekile, 2017), as an effective management policy in Nigeria in tackling the disease has not been in place.

It is worth noting that the poverty rate in Nigeria couple with emotional stress of the affected families is huge and therefore it would be impossible for some of the pharmacological and non-pharmacological therapies to be reached by carriers and families of the affected.

The rate of acceptability in managing the disease in newborn and antenatal diagnosis has been described in the findings as low; this is because of cultural background, religion and faith of the families' affected (Atkin et al.,2008).

Most carriers and familiesin Nigeria have the belief that cultural impact has a role in the acceptability of undertaking the associated diagnosis. Previous literatures indicate that, there exist difference in concept of health and diseases, such as; cause of the disease, acceptance of treatment and the type, reactions and so on. Such beliefs in Nigeria have a negative view and approach about the disease

(Anie et al., 2010) and this can obviously impact negatively on the management of the disease.

Also with respect to abortion upon diagnosis of the disease under prenatal screening of the unborn, it was observed that most of the studies identify carriers who are not willing to terminate such pregnancy on religious ground (Atkin et al., 2008).

Religion plays a prominent role in decision making in Nigeria, which consist of a large religious community who are committed to accepting whatever their faith direct them to do. The indication implies that if on a religious ground it was stated that a fetus that is diagnosed of the disease should not be terminated, by implication such will remain and in this case the purpose of the prenatal screening has been defeated as such management practice through this screening will not be allowed.

Awareness plays a major role in terms of enlightenment. It is human nature to fear the unknown especially a disease like sickle cell disease, which is dangerous and unpredictable. This could be terrifying regardless how factual the disease is.

Therefore, when carriers and families are aware of the management programs in place, with the implication involved, the need for a follow up of activities will be intensified.

Chapter 4

4.1 Conclusion and Recommendation

Sickle cell disease (SCD) globally has become a burden that covers a broad range of illness, which includesanemia and thalassemia. This occurs due to a sickle red shaped blood which alters the regular flow of hemoglobin leading to high health risk of death or disability.

SCD is most commonly found among people from sub-Saharan Africa, and the Asian continent and some part of the Mediterranean (WHO, 2005) and due to migration, it is now global.

In the global scene over 5% of the world population are carriers, with over 330,000 children born with it. In Africa, Nigeria has the highest burden, with over 150,000 children born with the disease annually and about 40 million carriers (Akinyanju, 2015), and this has call for concern.

However, literatures have shown that in the past decades, there has been tremendous improvement in the management of this disease because of medical advancement, which has led to reduction in mortality and morbidity rate and increase in the life expectancy and improvement in the quality of life of carriers, however this is most common in the developed and resourceful countries such as; the US and UK. Africa where the chief burden lies, the prevalence of the disease is still high, with less effort and concern by the government and health care practitioners.

Therefore, there is a huge call for an effective management that can impact the lives of carriers, however, in Africa and in Nigeria to be precise, the management has been inadequate and sub-optimal, and this has been a major challenge, but the question arises as to why this should be.

At this point, this systematic research indicated its objectives in chapter 1 to be;

Research objective one: To examine sickle cell management techniques in the health care settings in Nigeria.

In examining the management of sickle cell disease in Nigeria, Humphrey (2012), indicated that, the management of SCD could be classified as multifocal, multidisciplinary approach and in this sense, six management methods were examined, these are; Newborn screening,

Antenatal screening, clinical care of prenatal screening, clinical treatment of sickle cell disease, genetic counseling and the social environment.

Upon critical review of the relevant literature, it is observed that in the developed countries, these multifocal and multidisciplinary methods have been effective and these have helped in the reduction of mortality and morbidity rate and have also improve the quality of life of carriers, however in Nigeria, some of these methods are not fully established, such as newborn screening as a result of lack of facilities and infrastructure to carry out proper screening, high cost of treatment, and so on. It could have been better if these management methods are effectively in place in Nigeria.

Objective 2: To identify factors hindering the effective management of sickle cell disease in Nigeria

In each of the management methods identified, there are factors in the literature inhibiting their effectiveness in Nigeria, and these are categorized below;

Newborn screening,

- Lack of accuracy of self-report,
- Lack of facilities and infrastructure
- Lack of Acceptability
- Economic constraints

Antenatal screening

- Commitment to faith and religion

- Lack of knowledge
- Lack of prenatal diagnostic services
- Lack of Acceptability

Clinical care of prenatal screening

- Poverty
- Low standard of living

Clinical treatment of sickle cell disease

- High cost of treatment
- The perceived fear of actual and imaginary side effect of analgesic

Genetic counseling

- Lack of genetic education
- Religion
- Acceptability of result
- Fear of jettison

4.2 Recommendation

Based on the factors hindering the effective management of sickle cell disease in Nigeria as mentioned above, the following are hereby recommended;

- The programs for early detection of the disease should be properly established in the country with all necessary facilities and infrastructures in place.
- There should be transparency and trust by patient and family members on information provided with respect to SCD.
- There should be a joint prevention and treatment service in the health care planning program and the encouragement of existing initiative

- Regular Information collection on most suitable cost-effective approach for treatment and prevention should be encouraged in Nigeria
- There should be dedicated health care centers to make sure adequate services are available and rendered for an effective management.
- The government intervention ensuring all necessary policies and strategies to improve the quality of lives of carriers is urgently required.
- There should be highly educative centers to enable the enlightenment of carriers and family members to create awareness and for them to be well informed of the disease.

References

Adewoyin, A.S and Obieche, C (2015) Hypertransfusion therapy in sickle cell disease in Nigeria [Online] Availableat:<https://scholar.google.co.uk/scholar?hl=en&as_sdt=0%2C5&q=Adewoyin%2C+%282015%29+Hypertransfusion+therapy+in+sickle+cell+disease+in+Nigeria&btnG=>[Accessed 10th September 2017].

Adewoyin, A.S., Oghuvwu, O.S and Awodu, O.A (2017) Hydroxyurea therapy in adult Nigerian sickle cell disease: A monocentric survey on pattern of use, clinical effects and patient compliance [Online] Available at: https://www.ncbi.nih.gov [Assessed 24 November 2017].

Adeyemo, O., Omidiji, O and Shabi O.A (2007) Level of awareness of genetic counseling in Lagos, Nigeria: Its advocacy on the inheritance of sickle cell disease [Online] Available at: https://www.researchgate.net [Assessed 3rd December, 2017].

Akande, T.M. (2010), willingness of health workers to undergo premarital HIV screening Nigerian journal of hospital medicine [ejournal] Vol. 9 (4), p.303-306.http://dx.doi.org/10.4314/nqjhm.v9i4.12407.

Alege, L (2015) Sickle cell disease: Nigeria has the largest cases in the world [Online] Available at: http://www.vanguardngr.com [Assessed 15 November 2017]

Amstrong, T (N/A) Prevalence of sickle cell in Nigeria call for urgent attention-Obasanjo [Online] Available at: http://www.radionigerialagos.com [Assessed 15 November 2017]

Aneke, J.C and Okocha, C.E (2016) Sickle cell disease genetic counseling and testing: A review Journal of Archives of Medicine and Health science [ejournal]Vol.4, No.1, p.50-57.

Anie, K.A., Egunjobi, F.E and Akinyanju, O.O (2010) Psychosocial impact of sickle cell disorder: Perspectives from a Nigerian setting [Online] Available at: https://www.ncbi.nlm.nih.gov [Assessed 11 December, 2017]

Animasahun, A., Akintoye, C.O., Urowoli, N and Njokanma, O.F (2010) Premarital screening for sickle cell haemoglobin: awareness and acceptability among some categories of health professionals and medical students at the Lagos University Teaching Hospital [Online] Available at: https://www.researchgate.net [Assessed 30 November 2017]

Animasahun, A and Nwodo, U (2012) Prenatal screening for sickle cell anemia: awareness among health professionals and medical students at the Lagos University Teaching Hospital and the concept of prevention by termination Journal of Pediatrics and Hematology [ejournal] Vol.34 (4), p.252-256.

Ansong, D., Akoto, A.O., Ocloo, D. and Ohene-Frepong, K (2013) Sickle Cell Disease:

Management Options and Challenges in Developing Countries [Online] Available at: https://www.nih.gov [Assessed 3rd December 2017]

Atkin, K., Ahmed, S., Hewison, J and Green, J.M (2008) Decision-making and ante-natal screening for sickle cell and thalassaemia disorders [Online] Available at: https://www.researchgate.net [Assessed 3rd December 2017]

Asnani, M.R., Madden, J.K., Reid, L.G and Ayee, P.L Socio-environmental exposure and health outcomes among persons with sickle cell disease Journal of plos [ejournal] Vol.12 (4)

Burnham-Marusich, A. R., Ezeanolue, C.O., Obiefune, M.C., Yang, W., Osuji, A., Ogidi, A.G.,

Hunt, A.T., Patel, D and Ezeanolue, E.E (2016) Prevalence of Sickle Cell Trait and Reliability of Self-Reported Status among Expectant Parents in Nigeria: Implications for Targeted Newborn Screening Public health genomic [ejournal] Vol.2016 (19),p.298-306.

BwhThe management of patient with sickle cell: An overview [Online] Available at: <http://www.sickle.bwh.havard.edu> [Assessed 15th November 2017]

CDC (2017) Sickle Cell Disease (SCD) Complications and Treatments [Online] Available at: <http://www.cdc.gov> [Assessed 23rd November 2017].

Crosby, L.E., Barach, I., McGrady, M.E., Kalinyak, K.A., Esatin, A.R and Mitchell, M.J (2012).

Integrating interactive web based technology to assess adherence and clinical outcomes in pediatric sickle cell disease. Anemia 2012, 4924228

Fadare, J.O (2009) Some ethical issues in prenatal diagnosis of sickle cell anemia Annals of Ibadan post graduate Medicine [ejournal] Vol. 7(2), p.26-28.

Famuyiwa, O.O (2015) Sickle cell disorder: How do some people cope? Sickle cell bulletin [ejournal]Vol.6 No.1, p.3 -38.

FDA (2017) FDA approved L-glutamine powder for the treatment of sickle cell disease [Online] Available at: https://www.fda.gov [Accessed 24th November 2017]

Frommel, C., Brose, A., Klein, J., Blankenstein, O and Lobitz, S (2014) Newborn screening for sickle cell disease: Technical and Legal aspect of a German pilot study with 38,220 participants Journal of BioMed research International [ejournal]Vol.2014, No.695828, p.1-10.

Galadanci, N., Wudil, B.J., Balogun, T.M., Ogunride, G. O., Akinsulie, A., Hasan-Hanga, F., Mohammed, A.S., Kehinde, M.O ., Olaniyi, J.A and Diaku-Akinwumi, I.N (2014)Current sickle cell disease management practices in Nigeria International Health, Vol. 6, No.1, p.23–28

Gbeneol, P.K., Brisibe S.F and Odinioha, B (2015)Knowledge, Attitude and Uptake of Premarital Screening for the Sickle Trait among Married Couples in a Semi-Urban Community in South-South Nigeria European Journal of

Preventive Medicine [ejournal] vol.3(3), p.49-51.

Grove, J., Grove, O and Michie, C (2013) The real effects of sickle cell disease on Children and adolescent The West London Medical Journal [ejournal] Vol.6, No.1,p.11-17

Ham-Bolayi, W and Jordan, P (2016) Systematic review as a research method in post-graduate nursing education Health SA Gesondheid [ejournal]Vol.21 , p.120-128

Humphrey, G (2012)The management of sickle cell in primary care setting Journal of family medicine and primary care [ejournal] Vol. 1 No.1,p.56-58

Ibeagha, E.J and Ibeagha (N/A) Factors militating against acceptability of prenatal diagnosis of sickle cell anemia among health workers in selected hospitals in Anambra state[Online] Available at:https://www.globalacademicgroup.com[Assessed 7 December 2017]

Ikeanyi,E.M and Ibrahim, A.L (2014) Does antenatal care attendance prevent anemia in pregnancy at term? Nigerian Journal of Clinical Practice[ejournal] Vol.18 (3), p.323-327

Ilesanmi, O.O (2013) Sickle Cell Disease (SCD) and Stem Cell Therapy (SCT): Implications for Psychotherapy and Genetic Counseling in Africa [Online] Available at: https://www.intechopen.com [Assessed 8 December 2017]

Imhonde,H.O., Ndom, R.J.E., and Ehon, A (2013) Social support, Self esteem and depression as determinant of quality of life among sickle cell patients. Ife psychology [ejournal] Vol.21 (1), p.101-113.

Inusa, B.P., Daniel Y., Lawson, O., Dada, J., Mathews, C. E., Momi, S and Obaro, K (2015) Sickle cell disease screening in Northern Nigeria: The co-Existence of B-Thalassemia Inheritance [Online]Available at: https://www.omicsonline.org [Assessed 28 November 2017]

Isoa, E.M (2009) Current trends in the management of sickle cell disease: An overview Benin Journal of postgraduate medicine [ejournal] Vol.11 supplemental, p.50-64

Jacob, E., Stinson, J., and Zeltzer, L (2013) Remote monitoring of pain and symptoms using wireless technology in children and adolescent with sickle cell disease Journal of the America. [ejournal]

Jain, D., Lothe, A and Colah, R (2015) Sickle cell disease: Current challenges [Online] Available at: https://www.omicsonline.org [Assessed 7 December 2017]

Lane, P.A (2001) Newborn screening for hemoglobin disorder [Online] Available at: http://www.sickle.bwh.harvard.edu [Assessed 16 November 2017]

Marteau, T.M., Dormandy, E., Calnan, M.W., Atkin, K and Tsianakas, V (2012) Offering antenatal sickle cell and thalassaemia screening to pregnant women in primary care: A qualitative study of women's experience and expectations of participation Journal of Health expectations [ejournal]Vol.15, No.2, p.115-125

McBaun, M (2013) Sickle cell disease-Stroke prevention in Nigeria Trial (SPIN) [Online] Available at: https://www.clinicaltrials.gov [Assessed 5 December 2017]

Medline (2017) Prenatal care [Online] Available at: https://www.medlineplus.gov [Assessed 20 November 2017]

Medline (2017) Bone marrow transplant [Online] Available at: https://www.medlineplus.gov [Accessed 24 November 2017]

Memish, Z.A and Saeedi, M.Y (2011) Six years outcome of the national premarital screening and genetic counseling program for sickle cell disease and B-thalassemia

Mulumba, L.L and Wilson, L (2015) Sickle cell disease among children in Africa: An integrative literature review and global recommendations International Journal of Africa Nursing Science [ejournal] Vol.3 (2015), p.56-64

Ndukwu, G.U and Dienye, P.O (2012) Prevalence and socio-demographic factors associated with anaemia in pregnancy in a primary health centre in Rivers State, Nigeria Africa Journal of primary health care and family medicine[ejournal] Vol.4 (1), p. 328

NHS (2011) NHS Sickle cell and thalassaemia screening programme: Standards for the linked Antenatal and newborn screening programme [Online] Available at: http://www.sicklecellanemia.ca [Assessed 20 November 2017]

NHLBI (1995) Clinical Alert: Drug Treatment for sickle cell Anemia [Online] Available at: https://www.nlm.nih.gov [Assessed 23 November 2017]

NIH (2011) Sickle Cell Disease: Symptoms, Diagnosis, Treatment and Recent Developments [Online] Available at: http://www.medlineplus.gov [Assessed 20 November 2017]

Niihara, Y., Matsui, N.M., Shen, Y.M., Akiyama, D.A.,Johnson, C.S., Sunga, M.A., Magpayo, J., Embury, S.H., Kalra, V.K., Cho, S.H and Tanaka, K.R (2005) L-Glutamine therapy reduces endothelial adhesion of sickle red blood cells to human umbilica vein endothelial cell [Online] Available at: https://www.link.springer.com [Assessed 25 November 2017]

Odunvbun, M.E, Okolo, A.A, and Rahimy, C.M (2008) New born screening for sickle cell disease in Nigerian hospital- public health [Online] Available at: http://www.publichealthjrnl.com [Assessed 16 November 2017]

Ogundipe, S (2017) Pay more attention to sickle cell disease control, experts urge FG. [Online]

Available at: http://www.vanguardngr.com [Assessed 15 November 2017]

Okunola, M.A.,Olutayo, A.A., Okonkwo, N.S and Akingbola, T.S (2010) Pattern of contraceptive use among women with sickle cell disease in Ibadan, South-west Nigeria Journal of obstetrics and gynecology Vol.30(2)

Olatunya, O. Ogundare, E. O., Fadare, J., Oluwayemi, I.O., Agaja, O., Adeyefa, B and Aderiye, O (2015) The financial burden of sickle cell disease on households in Ekiti Southwest Nigeria Journal ofclinicoeconomics and outcomes research[ejounal] Vol. 2015(7),p.545-553

Oloyede, O.A., Olaide, A and Oyinye, N (2015) Clinical and laboratory experience of chorionic villous sampling in Nigeria Nigerian Journal of Clinical Practice Vol.17 (4),p.511-516

Oludarei, G. O (2013) Knowledge, Attitude and Practice of premarital counseling for sickle cell disease among youth in Yaba, Nigeria [Online] Available at:https://www.ncbinlm.nih.gov[Assessed 24 November 2017]

Omuemu, V.O., Obarisiagbon, O.E and Ogboghodo, E.O (2013) Awareness and acceptability of premarital screening of sickle cell disease among undergraduate students of the University of Benin Journal of Biomedical Sciences Vol. 1 (1)

Piety, Z.N., George, A.,Serrano, S., Lanzi, M.R., Patel, P.R., Noli, M.P., Kahan,S., Nirenberg, D.,

Camanda, J.F., Airewele, G and Shevkoplyas, S.S (2017) A paper –Based test for screening newborn for Sickle cell disease [Online] Available at: https://www.nature.com [Assessed 29 November 2017]

Robitaille, N., Delvin, E.E and Hume, H.A (2006) Newborn screening for sickle cell disease: A 1988-2003 Quebec experience [Online] Available at: http://www.ncbi.nlm.nih.gov [Assessed 16 November 2017]

Sansom-Daly, U.M., Peate, M., Wakefield, C.E., Bryant, R.A., and Cohn, R.J (2012) A systematic review of psychological interventions for adolescents and young adults living with chronic illness Health psychology Vol.31 (3), p.380-393

Short, M.E., Goetzel, R.Z., Pei, X., Tabrizi, M.J., Ozminkowski, R.J., Gibson, T.B., DeJoy, D.M and Wilson, M.G (2009) How Accurate are Self-Reports? An Analysis of Self-Reported Healthcare Utilization and Absence When Compared to Administrative Data Journal of occupational environmental medicine Vol.51 (7), p.786-796

Sinou, M.T(2017) Antenatal screening of sickle cell disease [Online] Available at: https://www.gfmer.ch [Assessed 20 November 2017]

Steinberg, M.H (1999) Management of sickle cell disease NEJM Vol.1999, No.340, p.1021-1030

Toni-Uebari, T.K and Inusa B.P.D (2009) The role of religious leaders and faith organization in haemoglobinopathies: A review [Online] Available at: https://www.ncbi.nlm.nih.gov [Assessed 24 November 2017]

Ugboma, H.A.A and George, I.O (2016) Sickle cell disease in pregnancy: Maternal and fetal outcome in Port Harcourt Nigeria British journal of medicine and medical research Vol. 7 No.1, p.40-44

Valenzuela,J.M., Vaughn, L.M., Crosby, L.E., Strong, H., Kissling, A., and Mitchell, M.J (2013) Understanding the experience of youth living with sickle cell disease: a photovoice pilot. Journal of Family community health [ejournal] Vol.36 (2), p.97-108

Vichinsky, E., Hurst, D., Earles, A.,Kleman, K and Lubin, B (1988) Newborn screening for sickle cell disease: Effect on mortality Journal of pediatrics [ejournal] Vol.81, No.6

Vichinsky, E.P (2017) Pregnancy in women with sickle cell disease [Online] Available at: https://www.uptodate.com [Assessed 22 November 2017]

WHO (2017) Sickle cell disease [Online] Available at: https://www.afro.who.int [Assessed 28 November 2017]

Yawn, B.P and John-Sowah, J (2015) Management of sickle cell disease: Recommendation from 2014 Expert panel report Journal of physicians [ejournal] Vol. 92(12), p.1069-1076

www.ingramcontent.com/pod-product-compliance
Lightning Source LLC
Chambersburg PA
CBHW071738090426
42738CB00011B/2524